ME

Animals in the Wild

Seal

by Mary Hoffman

Raintree Childrens Books
Milwaukee
Belitha Press Limited • London

This is a newborn harp seal. For the first few weeks of its life, it has a fluffy white coat, called "lanugo." Thousands of harp seal pups in Canada are killed for their white fur.

The baby seal drinks milk from its mother for the first few months of its life. Then it begins to catch and eat fish. These Weddell seals live in the Antarctic.

3

The most common seal is the harbor seal,
which lives in the North Atlantic. Seals spend a
lot of time in the sea but come up on the
beach to sunbathe.

Not all seals live where there are beaches.
These crabeater seals live in the Antarctic seas.
When they want to get out of the water, they
haul themselves up onto an ice floe.

The seal is well-suited for living in the water. It has a stream-lined body with flippers and a short, strong tail. Elephant seals and harbor seals have no outer ears. Fur seals and sea lions do.

Seals are wonderful swimmers and divers. But they have to come up for air sometimes. This Weddell seal can stay underwater for almost an hour. But then it must find a breathing hole in the ice.

Flippers help seals swim well, but they are not so useful for walking. Seals come out of the water to have their pups, but it takes them a long time to move up the beach.

This elephant seal is using her flippers in a different way—to cover herself with sand. It is a way of keeping cool on a hot day, while the seal is out of the water.

It is easy to see how the elephant seal got its name when you look at this male! It is a southern elephant seal, snoozing. It lives in the Antarctic with the penguins.

Male seals are larger than females. The
southern elephant seal is the largest of all
seals. The male may weigh 8,000 pounds,
almost four times as much as the female.

Sea lions belong to the eared seal family. They feel very much at home in the water. These are California sea lions, the kind that perform in circuses.

These two Galapagos sea lions are young
males. They are trying to find out which one is
stronger. The sea lion's front flippers are more
like legs than those of the earless seals.

Seals and sea lions come onto dry land to
mate and have babies. The big, dark sea lion is
the bull. The female cows are his mates. Each
cow usually has only one pup.

The newborn sea lion pup has tiny ears and
soft, brown fur. It is born with all its teeth, but it
is not yet ready to hunt for food. The pup grows
quickly from feeding on its mother's rich milk.

Sea lions that live in warm parts of the world,
like these on the California coast, may get too
hot even when they are in the water. So they use
their flippers like fans to cool themselves off.

But sometimes sea lions like to lie in the warm sun. It helps to dry out the layer of thick underfur that protects them against the cold when they are in the water.

This underfur is even thicker in the fur seals.
They are closely related to sea lions, as you
can see by the ears, but are smaller. This pup
will keep most of its fluffy fur when it grows up.

These young males look shaggy even when wet.
Fur seals live in the northern and southern
seas. These are from the Antarctic. All members
of the seal family like playing in the water.

Walruses may not look like sea lions and other seals, but they are closely related. Walruses spend a lot of time in the water, but give birth on beaches or on ice floes.

Walruses are very social animals. In this picture, hundreds of them have gathered on a rocky beach on an island in Alaska. If you look closely, you can see their long, white tusks.

Walruses are the only seals that have tusks.
Tusks are long, pointed teeth made of ivory.
Male walruses have very tough, bumpy skin.
These walruses are blushing to keep cool in
the hot sun.

Seals and sea lions are often friendly with people. But they eat a lot of fish, and that makes them unpopular with people who catch fish for a living. Many seals are killed because of this, as well as for their fur.

First published in this edition in the United States of America 1987
by Raintree Publishers Inc., 310 West Wisconsin Avenue,
Milwaukee, Wisconsin 53203.

First published in the United Kingdom under the title
Animals in the Wild—Seal
by Belitha Press Ltd.,
31 Newington Green, London N16 9PU
in association with Methuen Children's Books Ltd.

Library of Congress Number: 86-17806

Dedicated to Sanjana, Shamamah and Shabiba.

Scientific Adviser: Dr. Gwynne Vevers. Picture Researcher: Stella Martin.
Design: Ken Hatherley.

Acknowledgements are due to the following for the photographs used
in this book: Bruce Coleman Ltd pp. 1, 2, 5, 14, 15, 16, 18, 20, 22, 23
and front cover; NHPA p. 12; Oxford Scientific Films Ltd pp. 3, 7 and 13;
Frank Lane Picture Agency pp. 4, 8, 21 and back cover; Natural Science
Photos p. 6; Survival Anglia pp. 9, 10, 11 and 19; Eric and David
Hosking p. 17.

ISBN 0-8172-2702-4

Library of Congress Cataloging in Publication Data

Hoffman, Mary, 1945-
    Seal.

    (Animals in the wild)
    Summary: Portrays various kinds of seals and sea
lions in their natural environment and discusses
their struggle for survival.
    1. Seals (Animals)—Juvenile literature.
2. Sea lions—Juvenile literature.   [1. Seals
(Animals)   2. Sea lions]   I. Title.   II. Series.
QL737.P6H64   1987   599.74′6   86-17806
ISBN 0-8172-2702-4

1 2 3 4 5 6 7 8 9   90 89 88 87 86